COME ON IN!

Sharing the Good News through groups

A PRACTICAL ACTION GUIDE

MARGARET PARKER

METHODIST CHURCH HOME MISSION

First published 1993

ISBN 0 901015-09-1

Printed in Great Britain by
Warners (Midlands) plc, West Street, Bourne, Lincs, PE10 9PH

CONTENTS

PREFACE

My hope in writing this booklet is that ordinary Christians will stop feeling guilty about not sharing their faith with their friends, and will gain the confidence to try it.

And this is the time to do it! Not only are we into a Decade of Evangelism, but there is a great thirst in our land for spiritual things, as is apparent from the current disillusionment with materialism coupled with the growing interest in the occult, astrology, spiritism, and the New Age movement. Jesus Christ offers and is the meaning to life, and people need to hear about him!

Christianity is not a set of credal statements but an experience of a living Lord. Sharing our faith will be the natural outworking of that experience. By our lives we as Christian people will witness to the saving power and the practical love of Jesus Christ, so that our evangelism becomes spontaneous, ongoing and contagious.

This booklet is a resource; not everything in it will work for you, but it may be that something will fire you and provide the key to enable you to invite your friends to a small group where Jesus Christ is central.

Margaret Parker 1993

1 SETTING THE SCENE

'When the Holy Spirit comes upon you, you will be filled with power, and you will be witnesses for me in Jerusalem, in all Judaea and Samaria, and to the ends of the earth.'

Acts 1:8

My first experience of an evangelistic group was an afternoon at a friend's house chatting with a neighbour of hers about the Christian faith. There were only the three of us. We were there because the neighbour wanted to know how our ideas compared with those of the Jehovah's Witnesses who had visited her. We drank tea and talked about the difference Jesus makes. The meeting was informal, relaxed and enjoyable. We didn't cover all aspects of the gospel, nor did we challenge the neighbour to commitment. Her only response was a request to talk again. We met again the following week and she brought another friend along. I was excited and encouraged by the afternoon's events, and on reflection realised that some of my fears, sense of inadequacy and feelings of guilt about evangelism were evaporating. For me it was a beginning, as it was in a different way for the neighbour.

If it's so simple what stops us doing it?

That experience with my friend and her neighbour was certainly not too difficult! But I know very well that the prospect of being called upon to talk about our faith in a small group situation can be so intimidating that many of us will avoid it if possible. Housegroups for fellowship – fine! Housegroups for evangelism – no way!

So what gets in the way?

● **F-F-FEARS**

– that I will not know what to say
– that I will be tongue-tied even if I do know what to say!
– that I will be embarrassed
– that they will be embarrassed
– that I might be left to do it all on my own
– that they might not want to know

● **SENSE of inadequacy**

– my life does not live up to what I profess
– uncertainty about my beliefs

● **LOSS OF CONFIDENCE IN WHAT WE BELIEVE**

– they seem to have everything – do they really need God?
– they seem to have nothing – don't they really mostly need food and shelter?

- **MISCONCEPTIONS**
  – it needs a specialist to talk about faith
  – anyone who shares their faith needs to be able to talk a lot
  – evangelism is just for those who feel strongly about it

- **GUILT**
  I feel so guilty about not doing it that the guilt paralyses me

DON'T DESPAIR! We have probably all felt some or all of those things. Read on, gain ideas and confidence, and give it a try!

Let's be specific

It may be the word 'evangelism' that gets in the way, so let's try to define it ...

> 'One hungry person telling another hungry person where to find bread'

Evangelism is about making the Good News known.

So what is the Good News?

The Good News is that God made us and loves us. He came in human form to live and die for us. He offers us forgiveness and new life through Jesus Christ. He longs for us to respond to him in repentance, faith and love.

The Good News needs to be made known:-

- – clearly
- – simply
- – relevantly
- – starting where people are
- – offering only as much as they can take at a time
- – lovingly
- – non-judgementally

What motivates us to make the Good News known?

NOT a need to fill pews.
NOT a wish to have the most successful housegroup/fellowship/church in the neighbourhood.

BUT a heartfelt desire to enable others to find God through Jesus Christ – for their sakes, and for his.

All on my own?

NO – It's all done by TEAMWORK.

THE WHOLE CHURCH IS THE TEAM

We all use our differing gifts:-

some will offer their homes
some will make the coffee
some may write the invitations
some will invite friends
some will say what Jesus means to them
some may hire the video
some may point to a person who can answer the question

SOME are called to be evangelists. That is a special gift.

> 'Christ gave some to be apostles, some to be prophets, some to be evangelists ...' *Ephesians 4:11.*

ALL are called to be witnesses in one way or another.
A witness simply shares personal experience of the difference Jesus Christ makes.

THE CORPORATE LIFE OF THE CHURCH IS PART OF THE WITNESS

- The love of the members for each other.
- The care of the church as a whole for the community:
  - lunch club for the lonely
  - day centre for the housebound
  - open youth club for the teens
  - the warmth of the welcome to those who require the rites of passage, baptism, marriage, funeral.
- The message given by the appearance of the church:
  - noticeboard clear and welcoming
  - building and grounds well cared for
  - clear indication of how to get in
  - access for disabled people.
- The message given by those inside to any who venture in:
  - warm welcome, smile and handshake
  - offer of books (not too many!)
  - clear indication of where to go:-
  - for worship
  - for toilets
  - for Sunday School
  - for creche
  - etc ...

Why use small groups?

All small groups in the life of the church are potentially effective in introducing people to Jesus Christ. They have many positive features.

ADAPTABILITY

The small group is fully adaptable. It can meet at any convenient time of day, in any convenient venue. It can be any size, tackle any subject, use any method. A planned programme can be modified as required.

SENSE OF BELONGING

In the small group each person can feel valued, welcomed, accepted and heard. All of this promotes receptiveness.

FEEDBACK

Questions can be asked and answered. Points can be repeated for clarity. There is opportunity to hear what everyone thinks. Differing views can be safely expressed. People remember most when they have participated.

MINIMAL ORGANISATION REQUIRED

It can be done in a small way, with just one household involved. Inviting a few friends round to watch a video, meet a returned missionary or chat about the purpose of life is as simple as inviting them round to see our holiday slides. (But remember to pray a lot beforehand!)

MIX 'N' MATCH

A mix of three elements works well:- personal faith-sharing, small group for further discussion, the big event for teaching and sometimes challenge. The mix can be in any order, and any one can be repeated. The variety in presentation and the opportunity to meet other people contribute to a person's understanding and appreciation of what God is offering in Jesus.

All these features can help to draw people gradually and lovingly into faith. There is no need to know when it happened; after a while the evidence is there in changed attitudes, with a thirst for the word of God and for fellowship.

TO THINK ABOUT

- **What have I contributed in the last year to the teamwork of evangelism?**
- **What opportunities have I taken in the last year to talk about my faith?**
- **What opportunities have I missed?**
- **What has my church done in the last year to enable people to meet Jesus Christ?**
- **Is there anything God is calling me to do now?**

Write down anything you intend to do about it.

SOME BASIC PRINCIPLES

☐ It is God who converts. We help to create the climate.

☐ To communicate Christ *to* others we need to communicate *with* him ourselves. Back up everything with prayer.

☐ There is no one fail-safe method for effective evangelism.

☐ Evangelism is about meeting, not meetings; meeting other people where they are and enabling them to meet God.

☐ Start where people are rather than where you would like them to be.

☐ Listen first, to find out where they are!

☐ We are called to be faithful rather than successful in our witnessing. It's best to leave the results to God.

☐ In a loving presentation of the challenge of Jesus Christ to repentance and faith there is no room for manipulation, exploitation or compulsion.

☐ For evangelism to be effective we need each other.

- ☐ Expect things to happen.
- ☐ A small group can be anything from three to twelve people.
- ☐ A family is a small group.
- ☐ Responsible evangelism will ensure that provision is made for new Christians to be incorporated into the life of the church.

FAITH-SHARING IS NOT AN OPTIONAL EXTRA.

2 BUILDING BRIDGES

'Christ changed us from enemies into his friends and gave us the task of making others his friends also.'

2 Corinthians 5:18

Malcolm met Dave at the local badminton club. He soon discovered that Dave was something of a health fanatic. He was always at the gym, and was forever finding diets that would make him stronger, fitter, less prone to disease, or more likely to live longer. So when Malcolm's housegroup had on its programme 'A Christian doctor looks at health' it seemed natural for Malcolm to invite Dave along. It was there that Dave discovered that there's more to life than physical fitness, and that Jesus Christ offers a wholeness which embraces the physical, mental and spiritual.

This little cameo illustrates several useful points for us about making and taking opportunities by building bridges between Christians and the community, and about offering invitations to come and hear the gospel message.

Malcolm showed a genuine interest in Dave's interests.

Malcolm had been with Dave enough to know that health was vitally important to him. Being where people are is not just about going where they go and doing what they do, but about being alongside them in their *thinking*.

What are the major issues of the day?

What are the current philosophies?

What are the major local concerns?

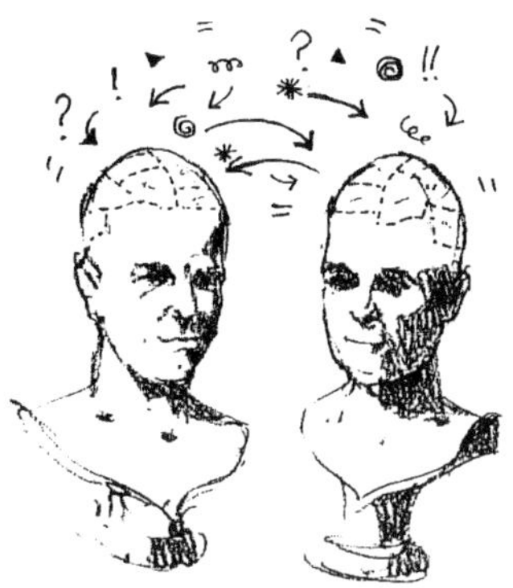

What are *your* friends most anxious about?

What newspapers do they read?

What TV programmes do they watch?

N.B. We will only be able to build bridges from the church into the community if we know where the community is, in its activities and in its thinking.

Malcolm chose to spend time on the other side of the bridge

Malcolm's relationship with Dave is sometimes referred to as pre-evangelism. And in a way that's what it is, in that it comes before the evangelism.

However, pre-evangelism sounds a bit deliberate and calculating, as if the sole purpose of getting to know people is ultimately to evangelise them. It may well be that sharing his faith with his friends was always somewhere in Malcolm's mind, but the relationship was much more about friendship, mutuality and shared interests – and that's one reason why the invitation to the housegroup was accepted. People can sense whether a friendship is genuine or whether there is a hidden motive.

How much leisure time do many Christian people spend building bridges and crossing them? Don't we tend to make the odd skirmish out there, perhaps for an evangelistic foray, and then retreat to the security of our church life and our church friends? And the keener we are, the more time we spend at church! We can't be salt in the community if all the salt stays together in one pile!

We don't need to do things we don't enjoy, but simply to pursue and develop our own interests within the community. But be warned – that may mean giving up some of our cherished jobs at church!

What about:

- evening/day classes
- clubs
- sport
- concerts
- amateur dramatics
- local politics
- over sixties ...?

The possibilities are endless.

It's not just individuals who can build bridges, but whole families. A number of churches are encouraging their families to spend regular time with non-church families, swimming, sharing barbecues, trips to the sea-side, the pantomime, the cinema, anything that families like to do together. Perhaps the children are friends from school, or the parents meet at the school gate or at the football match, or maybe they are all simply neighbours. Whatever the initial contact, there is great value in building bridges with whole families outside the church. It's thrilling to see a family come to faith together.

N.B. We cannot expect people to come across to the church side unless we have built a bridge which we are prepared to cross over to their side.

Consistent lifestyle

Malcolm was not perfect, but his lifestyle was good enough for Dave to take him seriously.

Once people know we are Christians they will notice our language, our attitudes, how we spend our time, how we spend our money, what we laugh at, what we watch on TV, what we read, how we face stress, illness, bereavement.

> *N.B. If we are to be credible witnesses our lives need to be transparently open, with nothing to hide. We don't want them to be unable to hear the message because of the lifestyle of the messenger.*

Malcolm had a network of relationships

Dave wasn't the only person Malcolm knew. There were other people, with different interests. If Malcolm had made a list of all the people he had contact with in a week, it would probably have been lengthy.

WE ALL HAVE A NETWORK OF RELATIONSHIPS

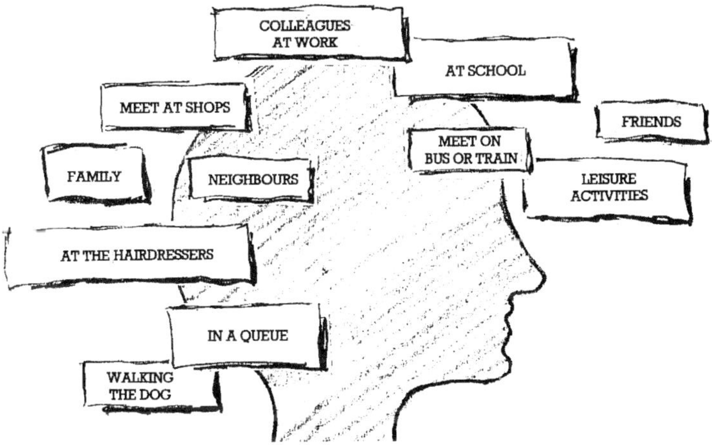

> *N.B. The bridges are in place. Do we expect two-way traffic?*

THE CHURCH HAS A NETWORK OF RELATIONSHIPS

COMMUNITY ROLL/USERS OF PREMISES

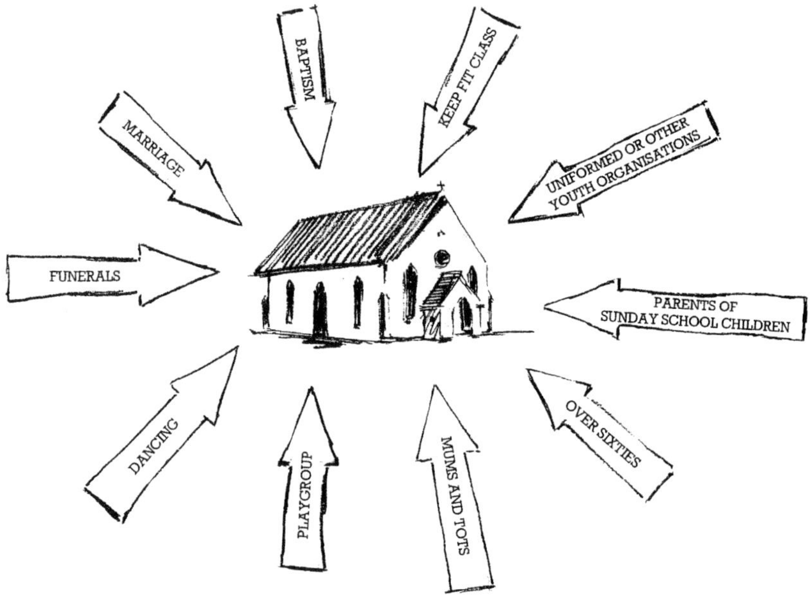

> *N.B. These people from outside have built bridges to the church.*
>
> *What impression of the church do they get?*

Malcolm was expecting opportunities to invite Dave over the bridge

When we used the *Person to Person* course on evangelism training in our church, it was noticeable that people who one week said that no opportunities for talking about their faith ever came their way, suddenly the week after the discussion had all sorts of opportunities.

> *N.B. We do not notice opportunities unless we are expecting them!*

KEY POINTS TO REMEMBER

- ☐ Genuine interest, care and concern for people will build the best bridges.
- ☐ We cannot expect people to cross over to our side of the bridge unless we are prepared to cross over to theirs.
- ☐ Be clear and honest about what you are inviting them to.
- ☐ Our lives need to recommend the gospel we proclaim.
- ☐ We need to be aware of our network of relationships.
- ☐ We need to be prepared to seek and take opportunities to invite our friends to appropriate groups.
- ☐ The life and message of our church (noticeboards, magazine, attitudes of members) need to recommend the gospel to the people who use the premises week by week.

TO THINK ABOUT

During the week make a list of the people with whom you have regular contact.

- **What are their main interests?**
- **Is there any way I can share their interests?**
- **Are there any families who could join up with non-church families for activities?**

During the week make a list of the people who regularly use your church premises.

- **What must be their impression of the church?**
- **Is there anything I can do to give them a better impression?**
- **Is there any way I can get to know them better?**

Write down anything you intend to do about it.

3 THE INVITATION

'Always be prepared to give an answer to everyone who asks you to give the reason for the hope that you have. But do this with gentleness and respect.' *1 Peter 3:15*

Scratch where it itches
In the previous chapter Malcolm waited for an opportunity to invite Dave to a meeting he knew Dave would be interested in. There are many ways to faith in Jesus Christ. Coming in has been likened to entering an arena through one of many passages.

Some will enter through bereavement, others through the birth of a child, others through illness, or concern for the world, or the need to belong, or to be loved, or to find forgiveness, or through anxiety about their children, or the desire for wholeness, or truth, or purpose in life, or because of fear of death. All come ultimately to Christ, but the entrance point is different.

> *N.B. We need, then, to lead our friends to the right entrance for* them.

This may mean waiting a while until a suitable occasion arises to invite them to a meeting. Of course, there is nothing to stop us talking to them meanwhile, and we will do that. But it's worth waiting for the right moment to introduce them to a group.

Small groups as staging posts

People who have not been inside a church for years naturally feel nervous about going. Where do they sit? When should they stand up and sit down? Will they be able to follow what is happening?

The small group, wherever it meets, is for many people less threatening, offers opportunity to ask questions, and enables new people to feel their way in gently.

It must be said, however, that for some the small group is intimidating and they prefer the relative anonymity of a church service.

So we need to be sensitive to our friends' needs and feelings. We can offer the small group as a staging post for people to test the water and take time to decide whether to go any further.

Be natural

'I'm going to a friend's house tonight to ... Care to come with me?'
'We're inviting a few friends round to ...'
'There's this really interesting chap speaking about ... Want to hear him?'
'We're having a discussion at the housegroup tonight about ...'

Give clear information

'It's a video about the meaning of Christmas, and we'll all be able to say what we think afterwards. Mind you, no one *has* to speak! It starts at 8.00, and it's across at Ann and Pete's. Mary and Bill are going, and probably Ian and Sally with Jenny. It will end by 10.00. We can call for you about ten to eight if you want to come.'

Give a choice

Never embarrass people or put them on the spot. Make it possible for them to decline the invitation without loss of face. 'Are you interested, or have you got other plans for that night?' Indicate that you think they will be interested but do not coerce them.

No strings attached

If they come with you once, they must not be made to feel that they have committed themselves for ever, or that they will let you down if they do not want to come again.

It's useful to have a further meeting on offer for those who are especially interested, but to make it clear that not everyone is expected to come again.

Be honest

Avoid getting anyone to a meeting under false pretences; they will respect neither you nor your message.

KEY POINTS TO REMEMBER

- ☐ Excessive enthusiasm can be off-putting!
- ☐ It's about teamwork.
- ☐ Some will find it natural to chat with non-Christian friends about the difference Jesus makes in their lives, others will prefer to invite them to a Christian meeting. We need both!
- ☐ You are not inviting them to hear the whole of the gospel message in one evening. Don't expect instant conversion!

TO THINK ABOUT

During the week make a list of your friends who are not yet part of the church.

- **Is the list longer or shorter than I expected?**
- **Is there any Christian group which would be of particular interest to any of my friends?**
- **Is there anybody I could invite to go with me to:**
  - **a Christian concert.**
  - **hear a well-spoken speaker.**
  - **a special service.**
  - **a Christian holiday?**

Write down anything you intend to do about it.

4 LAUNCHING THE GROUP

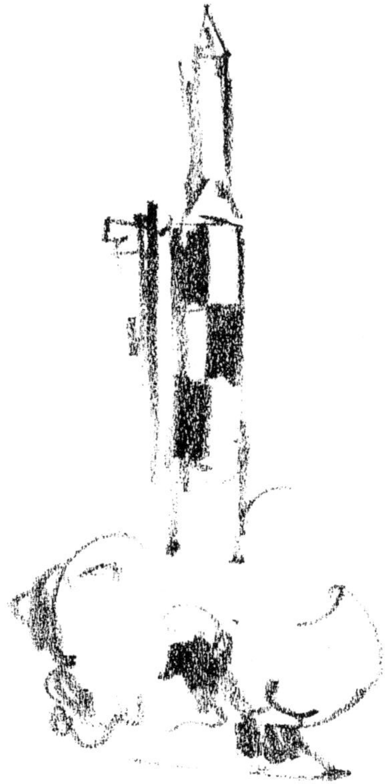

'I believed; therefore
I have spoken'
2 Corinthians 4:13

Mary was walking home with a neighbour from a friend's funeral. The neighbour was telling Mary of her fears about death and dying, and Mary was able to say a little about how her Christian faith took away her fear of being dead, though she admitted to being a bit afraid about how she would face up to the process of dying. When they reached Mary's gate, the neighbour remarked that she would like to hear a bit more about what Christians believe about the life after death, and Mary agreed to meet her to chat again the next afternoon. Back in the house, Mary panicked. What did she really know about it? How could she help? She would never be able to answer her neighbour's questions! How she longed to have a small group to which she could invite her neighbour where others could share in the conversation. But there was nothing like that in her church.

If Mary had the courage to set up a group, how could she go about it?

When?
Whenever the people you want to invite are available! Think creatively. 7.45 pm is not the only time!

Mornings or afternoons for retired people, mornings or early afternoons for mums. At lunchtime you might provide soup and bread. How about early evening with a meal for families? Saturdays or Sunday afternoons might be best for singles, families, or business people.

What format?
Groups may be formal or informal. A few friends chatting together will suit some, a meeting with a speaker and opportunity for questions will suit others.

Refreshments are helpful especially at the beginning of the first meeting. Coffee at the end offers opportunity for informal conversation about the content of the meeting.

How?
For an informal get-together, word of mouth will be adequate,

though the bare details on a slip of paper will be a useful reminder.

For a more formal group, use printed/typed/written cards with full details, backed up by personal invitation. (Christian Publicity Organisation, Worthing produce attractive cards with an optional overprinting service).

Planning

Be in on the planning
It's helpful to become involved at the outset in the planning of groups for evangelism. Then you can ensure that what is proposed will be of interest to *your* friends.

Be ecumenical
If possible work with Christians from other local churches. Ecumenical evangelism conveys a healthy message to the community.

Dimension or intention?
All groups within the life of the church will have an evangelistic *dimension;* it *should* be possible to find faith and become part of the church through any church group! Some groups will be set up with a specific evangelistic *intention.*

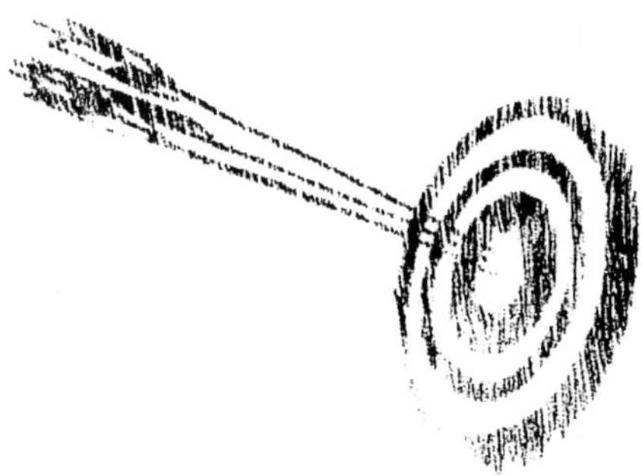

Keep your aim in mind
Your overall aim in groups with an evangelistic intention will be to bring people to a living faith in God through Jesus Christ. Don't lose

sight of that through complicated structures or organisation, through power struggles or status seeking, or through motives such as filling pews or raising money.

Have clear and specific objectives
Do not try to convert the whole community in one year! Your objective may be sharing the gospel with the people who live around the church or with friends and contacts of church members or with those who have a link with the church through baptism, marriage, funerals, children's activities.

Pray
Pray for God's guidance in every detail, and for wisdom, sensitivity and love.

Practicalities

Who to invite?
You need to invite a mix of Christians and others and an appropriate number for the size of the room. Your specific objective will provide the target group. Decide whether to include a variety of ages and interests, or to have a homogeneous group; for instance, all young couples, all neighbours, all over-60s, all parents of teens. It's helpful to have at least one thing in common.

Who invites them?
It may be the hosts, or each Christian brings a friend or the minister invites couples who have had their babies baptised. Don't all leave it to someone else.

Where?
You will need an accessible building, comfortable chairs, adequate heating, ventilation and light, toys if children are around, offers of transport or babysitting.

It's natural to invite them to *our* house and that may be right. Or you could offer to meet in the home of one of the newcomers where they would feel more relaxed. (This is the approach of the *Good News Down the Street* evangelism. Grove booklet, available from Christian bookshops).

To avoid the need for babysitters or transport you could meet in the home of young parents or housebound.

In some situations homegroups may not be appropriate, and the coffee lounge at the church would be better, or a room in the local pub or wherever people are accustomed to meet.

Presentation

Feelings
Be aware of your visitors' feelings as they arrive (uncertainty, fear, embarrassment, unease?).

Activity
Help them to relax by providing something to do:- offer coffee, tea, or any other drink ('Come round for a drink' may not be recommended Methodist practice, but the method is a very good ice-breaker!). Introduce each to one or two others, mentioning anything they have in common. Leave attractive books, leaflets, pictures lying around to provide a talking point.

Have fun
Create the impression that we are all here to enjoy this together, rather than that something is going to be imposed on them for their good.

Speak naturally
Your Christian faith is an integral part of your life and does not require a different voice or stance when you talk about it. Use everyday language; try to avoid religious jargon.

Small numbers
Do not apologise if numbers are small.

No pretence
If it is clear that only Christians are present, abandon the programme, talk and pray! Don't keep up a pretence of doing evangelism if that's not what it is.

Prayer?
It may embarrass people if you say a prayer at the beginning. Depending on how the meeting has gone it may be helpful to close with one.

Get going
As soon as possible start the advertised programme; waiting for something to happen can make adults uneasy and children restless.

Questions
Give opportunity for question and comment, and take seriously whatever is said, without appearing patronising, critical or judgmental.

Show respect
If people do not want to talk, respect their choice.

No arguments
Put your point of view, but do not argue.

Be true to your word
Do not spring any surprises. Limit yourself to what is on the invitation.

Follow-up meeting
If it seems right, suggest another meeting for those who want to explore the subject further, but put no pressure on anyone.

Free to stay or go
Finish at the stated time. If some want to stay and talk, provide another drink, making it clear that it will not be discourteous for people either to leave or stay.

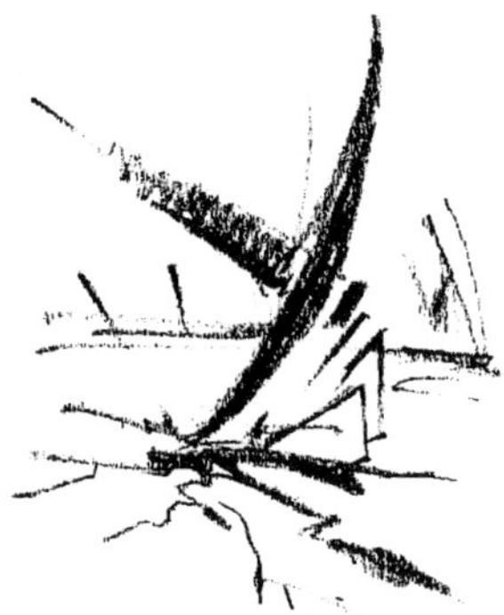

USEFUL ICE-BREAKERS FOR INFORMAL GROUPS

(Not to be used where people prefer to listen rather than talk)

(A) Ask each person first to sit with and talk to someone they do not know very well and then to introduce them to the group.

(B) For those expecting a discussion, four questions:

Where did you live when you were aged about 7?

What did you play with?

What/who was the place of warmth and security in your life?

What was your first awareness of God/any power greater than human?

Everyone briefly answers question one, then everyone answers question two, and so on. If any prefer simply to listen, respect their choice. The smaller the group, the quicker the exercise. Follow it up by sharing how your experience of God has changed since then, or move on to whatever programme you have planned.

KEY POINTS TO REMEMBER

Small group evangelism should ...

- ☐ be serious but not without laughter.
- ☐ be about Jesus Christ but not everything about him in one meeting.
- ☐ address the deep questions of life but not take everyone out of their depth.
- ☐ offer a challenge to response but not force it.
- ☐ never accuse, judge or frighten.

TO THINK ABOUT

- **Are there any groups in my church with an evangelistic intention?**
- **Which church leaders can I talk to and pray with about forming/developing evangelistic groups?**
- **Which other Christians in my church or other churches around are likely to be interested?**
- **Which particular people/group of people do we feel a special concern for?**
- **Where could we meet?**
- **Who would introduce the meeting?**
- **Would it be formal or informal?**
- **Who would decide on the programme?**

Write down anything you intend to do about it.

5 BIBLE ENCOUNTER

Why use the Bible?

We use the Bible for evangelism because:

- God speaks through it.
- people can encounter Jesus Christ through reading it.
- it gives a focus to a discussion.
- the gospel message is implicit in it, and explicit in some parts.
- using it with non-Christians shows that we are not merely quoting our own opinions.
- it deals with real-life situations.

Do's and Don'ts

DON'T – arrive with large ostentatious Bibles under your arm.

- assume that people can quickly find their way around the Bible.
- ask newcomers to read aloud, or have people 'reading round'.
- always start by reading a Bible passage. Lead the group into the subject matter from where they are.
- patronise, assuming total ignorance. If you are unsure whether they will know some relevant fact, include it with the words, 'You will probably know...'
- show shock at what people say.
- get into arguments.

DO – encourage them to come with an invitation such as 'I find it helpful to discuss the Bible with other people. Would you like to give it a try?'

– let them know what they are coming to. Is it a one-off, or part of a series?

– plan a series two or three times per year so that Christians always have an evangelistic Bible study to which they can invite friends.

– join with other churches in the circuit or locality to make it viable.

– encourage the Christians in the group to mingle with the others.

– have several attractive Bibles available. The Bible Society produce separate gospels.

– let the Bible speak for itself. It does not need us to defend it.

– keep praying.

This chapter contains:-

(a) A Bible study for Christians to prepare them for sharing their faith.

(b) A series of four studies on the life of Peter, for people exploring faith.

(a) and (b) illustrate different methods of Bible study. These methods are offered as a resource to use in other studies. Appendix One contains another ten series of Bible studies in brief outline.

For further ideas

(i) see *Leading Groups: A Training Course,* Margaret Parker, Epworth Press, 1987.

(ii) *Good News Down The Street,* Grove booklet, offers a method for homegroup evangelism and six study outlines on Jesus.

A. Bible study for Christians

AIM

To give a small group of Christians knowledge of and confidence in the message of the gospel to enable them to share it.

ICE-BREAKER

Each write in one sentence what the gospel is. Compare answers. Re-read each sentence through the eyes of a non-Christian known to you with whom you would like to share the gospel. What will they understand by it? Will it seem relevant to their situation? Are there technical words which need expressing in non-technical terms?

BIBLE INPUT

1. The message in story form

Read Luke 15:11-32.

Form three groups (or multiples of three if you have large numbers). Each group explore the feelings of one of the participants at each stage of the story – father, younger son, elder son. After ten minutes, put all the findings on a chart (wall or floor) under the three headings.

Add to the chart who you think Jesus meant each of the three to represent:- father: God; younger son: tax collectors and outcasts (see verse 1); elder brother: Pharisees and teachers of the Law (verse 2). Discuss who each represents today. What do we learn about God? ... and ourselves?

N.B. This is also a challenging passage to use with the uncommitted

2. The message explained

Who is Jesus? Read 1 Corinthians 15:3-5 and Colossians 1:15-20. List and discuss all that we learn about Jesus, the heart of our message.

3. The message in picture language

Look up the following references and note the different images used to describe what is involved in being a Christian.

Ephesians 2:5	From death to life.
2 Corinthians 5:20	From enemies to friends.
John 9:39	From blindness to sight.
Luke 19:10	Saved.
John 3:3	Born again.
Ephesians 4:22-24	Putting off old self and putting on new.
Romans 5:1	Peace with God.
Romans 8:1	No condemnation.

If you have time, add others to the list. Thinking of people with whom you would like to share your faith, which of these images would be most helpful to their situation?

REFLECTION

Look again at your original one-sentence gospel. Do you want to modify it?

Pray for yourselves, for a sense of urgency, for understanding, clarity, sensitivity, compassion …

Pray for your friends, that they will respond to what God has done for them in Christ.

B. A series of four studies on the life of Peter – for those exploring faith

Study 1. The Call. Luke 5:1-11

Have enough New Testaments for everyone, or if people are not used to handling books, duplicate the verses on single sheets. Pass them round after the ice-breaker.

ICE-BREAKER

Imagine someone rang to ask you to go and work for him. What would it take to make you go? Each jot down or call out your thoughts. Leader compile on a chart a list of all suggestions. Put the list on one side until later.

BIBLE INPUT

Someone asked a man called Simon to leave his job and follow him. Read aloud Luke 5:1-11.

Questions to discuss either in full group if not more than eight, or in threes and fours.

Describe how you think Peter was feeling at each stage. What made him realise he was sinful? What did he mean by that? Why did he tell Jesus to go away from him?

What sort of person do you think Jesus was, that people left everything and followed him? Are there any ways in which we are similar to Peter? Put all answers to last two questions on separate wall charts, or on large cards on the floor where everyone can see them. If appropriate, ask how members of the group feel about Jesus, and whether they want to follow him.

OTHER SUGGESTIONS FOR OPENING UP THIS PASSAGE

1) Character studies. Brainstorm (i.e. call out everything that comes to mind) on to a wall/floor chart all you know or can deduce from this passage about (a) Peter and (b) Jesus. Looking at what is written up, would you like to meet Peter? Why/why not? Would you like to meet Jesus? Why/why not?

2) In pairs, re-read the passage. After discussion, one be the interviewer and interview the other as Peter asking what happened and how he felt about it. One pair may like to enact the interview for the rest of the group.

3) Working in pairs, imagine one of you is Simon Peter, the other Jesus, and re-read verse 4 where Jesus tells Simon to let down the nets. From that point let the conversation develop in as many different ways as you can. Some may like to share their dialogue with the group.

All together again, re-read verses 4-11 to remind yourselves of what actually happened.

TO PULL THE THREADS TOGETHER

Look back at your list of what it would take to make you go and work for someone. Which, if any, of these does Jesus offer? What else does he offer?

Study 2. Up and Down. Matthew 16:13-23

ICE-BREAKER

Either (a) give out pieces of paper and pens and ask each person to draw a graph of one or two high spots and low spots in their lives. (It will help if you have prepared yours in advance and can show it to them). It could look like this.

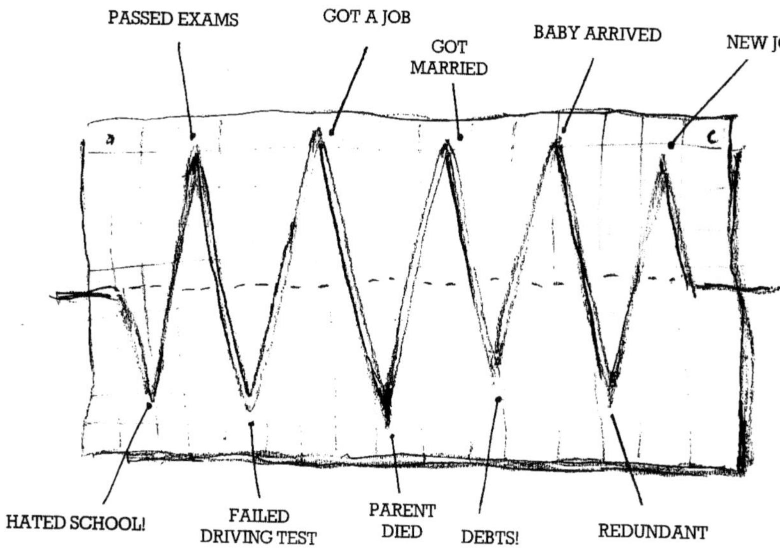

Members may like to explain their graph to one or two others.

Do not insist.

Or (b) ask what answers you might expect if you were to ask people in a local pub who they think Jesus was or is.

BIBLE INPUT

Questions for verses 13-20:-

Who did people say Jesus was?

Who did Peter say Jesus was?

Who do we say he is?

Questions for verses 21-23:-

Why did Jesus say he was going to die?

Why was he going to die?

Why was he angry with Peter?

What has his death to do with us?

OTHER SUGGESTIONS FOR OPENING UP THE PASSAGE

1) Character studies. Continue building up the character studies of Peter and Jesus begun in study 1. Is there anything about Jesus that strikes you as being different from most people?

2) In twos and threes write a postcard that Peter could have sent home to his wife after this incident.

3) In very small groups talk about times when you have felt like Peter probably felt at any stage in this incident.

4) Watch the video *Crucifixion* in the *Jesus Then and Now* series.

TO PULL THE THREADS TOGETHER

If you did ice-breaker (a) each indicate on your graph any point at which Jesus meant something to you.

If you did ice-breaker (b) talk about how you yourself would now describe Jesus.

Study 3. Denial.
Matthew 26:31-35, 69-75

ICE-BREAKER

Describe, either in the full group or in twos and threes an occasion when you have (a) let someone down (b) been let down.

BIBLE INPUT

Read the passages, and add a summary of verses 36-68.

Questions for verses 31-35:-

What made Peter so sure that he would not deny Jesus?

What made Jesus so sure that he would?

Questions for verses 69-75:-

List Peter's feelings at each stage.

How would we have reacted if we had been there?

How would we have felt about our reactions?

Is there anything we can do to Jesus that he cannot forgive?

OTHER SUGGESTIONS FOR OPENING UP THE PASSAGE

1) Character studies. Continue with the character studies of Peter and Jesus from previous studies.

2) Discuss what you would have liked to have said to Peter if you had met him immediately after verse 75. What do you think Jesus would have said to Peter if he had talked to him then?

3) In three groups, one group discuss the actions and feelings of Peter, one of Jesus, and one of the servant girls and onlookers. Each group tell the other groups what happened in the incident and how it felt.

If appropriate encourage one from each group to act it out.

TO PULL THE THREADS TOGETHER

Discuss in what ways, if at all, you feel like Peter.

Study 4. Reinstatement.
John 21:1-19

ICE-BREAKER

Either (a) List the characteristics you would want to find in a leader of a new organisation you planned to join.

Or (b) Look at the 'graffiti' on the 'wall'. (Reproduce on a large card).

JESUS IS

troublemaker ... friend ... forgiver ... challenger ... dead ... alive ...
God ... healer ... mad ... never lived ...

Discuss which of these is the nearest to your experience.

BIBLE INPUT

The passage could helpfully be read as a dialogue.

Questions for discussion:-

Why did Jesus say something similar three times?

How do you think Peter would have been feeling at each stage?

How would we have felt?

OTHER SUGGESTIONS FOR OPENING UP THE PASSAGE

1) Character studies. Complete them. What picture do we get of Peter? of Jesus?

2) Describe a situation in which a freedom fighter is taken prisoner and his second-in-command when questioned denies any knowledge of him. How might their conversation go when the freedom fighter is released?

3) Watch the video *Resurrection* from the *Jesus Then and Now* series.

TO PULL THE THREADS TOGETHER

If you did ice-breaker (a) discuss how Jesus measures up to your ideal picture of a leader.

If you did ice-breaker (b) discuss any ways in which your ideas have changed since you started this series.

TO CONCLUDE THE SERIES

Thinking back over Peter's experiences, are there any things that strike a chord in your experience?

Any things you have learned about yourself? About Jesus?

What sort of relationship do you have/would you like to have with Jesus?

Anything you want to do about it?

Close the series with prayer, and offer to talk privately to anyone who wants to explore further.

6 ADDITIONAL THINGS TO DO

> Day after day they met as a group in the temple and they had meals together in their homes eating with glad and humble hearts, praising God, and enjoying the goodwill of all the people. And every day the Lord added to their group those who were being saved. *Acts 2:46-7*

- A speaker – or series of speakers – with a speciality. For example: My faith and my career in:- business/teaching/ medicine/politics/sports/music/advertising.
- Interview with a prominent local Christian.
- Question Time to a panel of Christians. Any subject you like, but here's one suggestion:- Things you have always wanted to know about Christianity but have never liked to ask.
- Informal gathering with a focus:- to meet a visiting overseas Christian, to discuss a recent TV programme, to watch and discuss a video, to discuss a current event, to sing carols.
- A small dinner party with discussion or after-dinner speaker.
- A buffet/fish and chip/pea and pie supper followed by video/speaker/discussion.
- Drop-in Christian book-party with occasional book reviews and discussion (books can be obtained by book agents with Christian bookshops on a sale or return agreement).
- Drop-in Traidcraft/Tearfund party with opportunity for discussion on Third World issues.
- Show slides of the Oberammergau Passion Play to lead into a

discussion about the meaning of the Cross.

- Family film/video in public hall followed by discussion/activities in age groups.
- Family outing/picnic/party followed by epilogue.
- Prepare and take out to neighbouring houses a questionnaire on people's attitudes to God. Follow up with a meeting to discuss the findings.
- A banner-making group in which discussion and Bible study precede the designing and making of banners.
- A regular homegroup can have the occasional Open (evangelistic) Meeting to which members invite their friends.
- Meetings in which Christians and others share in conversation on Christian issues.

Conversation-starters:-

- What excites you? angers you? frightens you?
- Who do you think Jesus was and is?
- Do you believe that God cares what happens in the world?
- What is important to you?
- What do you think happens when we die?
- How do you think the world will end?
- What's gone wrong with the world?

The day's newspapers can provide subject-matter for discussion.

E.g. circulate mounted newspaper articles which demonstrate the fallenness of human nature and discuss whether anyone is perfect, what is sin, is there hope for the world, etc ...

- Other topics and titles:-
  - Answering children's questions about God.
  - Why I became a Christian.
  - A Christian doctor looks at life.

- The occult and the Christian gospel.
- The New Age and the Christian gospel.
- Heavy metal and the Christian gospel.
- Islam and the Christian gospel.
- Why suffering?
- Family life in the 90s – where is it going?
- Is marriage out of date?
- Grandads for God: life after 65.
- Is there life before death? A Christian viewpoint.
- What is a Christian?
- Does Christianity make sense?
- Christian viewpoint: an overall title with several slants.

● Brainstorm on who Jesus was and is.

1. Write swiftly on a large piece of paper everything everyone remembers about Jesus.

Use one word where possible for each idea.

(Don't worry if some ideas are not exactly right; there will be opportunity later to check things out in the Bible).

2. When the paper is full, or people dry up, identify words referring to his birth, his ministry, his death, his resurrection and his ascension.

(It can be useful to circle words with felt pens, one colour for each subject).

3. Talk about his birth.

Look up a few short Bible passages to amplify, clarify and perhaps correct what is on the chart. Try to concentrate on the wonder and mystery of the birth, and its significance for us. Make a list for use in a future meeting of issues which need more time.

4. Talk about his ministry. Look up one or two Bible passages which pick up the points from the chart. Again make a list of aspects which people want to explore further.

5. Talk about his death, then his resurrection and ascension in the same way, concentrating on what it can mean to us.

6. Allow time for questions, and note down any which can be taken up at a later meeting.

Because the whole meeting has arisen out of ideas brought by the group, they are likely to be receptive and open to discover more.

By the end of the meeting you will have material for a series on the Person and Work of Jesus Christ.

If appropriate, you may like to hand out lists of Bible passages for reading at home or to prepare for a follow-up meeting.

KEY POINTS TO REMEMBER

- ☐ God is interested in everything that concerns people.
- ☐ The gospel has something to say about everything that concerns people.
- ☐ Start where people are and demonstrate the relevance of the gospel to their situation.
- ☐ Some will come because they are interested in the subject, others because they are interested in and may want to argue about what Christians have to say about the subject. Don't expect everyone to be at the same starting point.

TO THINK ABOUT

- **What subjects are my friends interested in?**
- **What particular needs are they expressing at the moment?**
- **What does the gospel have to say about that?**
- **What would be the best approach to enable them to realise the relevance of the gospel?**

Write down anything you intend to do about it.

7 THE CHALLENGE TO COMMITMENT

To all who received him, to those who believed in his name, he gave the right to become children of God *John 1:12*

One week at the homegroup, Penny asked if she could say something. There were murmurs of encouragement from other group members, and Penny continued. "Well, when Sarah first invited me here I wasn't too sure that I wanted to come. Anyway, I came, and gradually I got to know you all and I felt that you really cared about me – especially that day when I'd lost my dog and you all went out looking for her. You seemed to know Jesus in a kind of personal way and I couldn't understand that. I knew a bit about *Jesus from Sunday School and things, but he wasn't real to me like he was to some of you. Then the other week we were talking about Jesus being the*

vine and us the branches. I suddenly realised that I had to do *something about it, but I didn't know what. Then last week, Mary, you said that we need to make a decision about Jesus, whether to accept him or reject him, and it struck me that I needed to accept him. So I took one of those little books home – you know, the ones you left on the coffee table – and that night I read it, and said the prayer at the end. I asked Jesus to forgive me and to take over my life. And I'm sure he did. It's taken a long time, but I was ready for that little push 'cos I tend to put things off if I can. So I really just want to say thank you to you all."*

Penny's group got it right! They welcomed her, cared for her, spoke naturally about Jesus, spelt out the need for a decision to be made and provided her with the means of doing it.

Of course, not everyone consciously makes a decision like that. Some people realise only as they look back that Jesus has become real, that he is their Saviour, that they have a relationship with God as Father and that the Holy Spirit is at work in their lives. They cannot put a date on it.

Why is a challenge necessary?

Many of us tend to duck out of offering challenges to people. That may be because we do not want to force them, or because we are afraid they will not respond. We will be letting them down badly if after presenting the gospel through Bible study, testimony, talk, video or whatever, we allow them to go away not knowing what they can do about Jesus.

The fact that Christ died for all does not mean that all are automatically forgiven. Each person needs to make an individual response.

The challenge is *implicit* in what God has already done in Christ; our task is to make it *explicit* by offering people the opportunity to respond to what he has done for them.

The response

The response is the acknowledgement that God has done everything for us because we could not do it for ourselves. It is the offering of ourselves to him in repentance and surrender. The person who makes such a response becomes a Christian.

There are many ways of describing what happens. Use whichever you are comfortable with. Some terms focus on our activity: accepting Christ, committing our lives to Christ, receiving new/eternal life, asking Christ to come into our lives.

Other terms focus on what happens to us when we respond: being converted, being born again, being saved, being redeemed.

However it is described, becoming a Christian is a gift which God has bought for us by the death of Christ.

How do we offer the challenge to commitment?

The challenge may be offered by the host, another member of the group, or a visiting speaker. It is helpful to have other mature Christians around to observe people's reactions and to be available to chat to them afterwards.

Towards the end of the group meeting, speak to the group about the need at some point to make a decision. Make it clear that not everyone will necessarily want to do this just now. Stress that there is a choice. Explain that to enter into a relationship with God we need to talk to him. Say a simple prayer along these lines. Pause between sentences, asking people to echo it in their minds if they mean it.

Dear God, I know I have done wrong.

I am truly sorry.

I believe that you love me and want to forgive me.

Jesus Christ, thank you for dying so that I can be forgiven.

Please come into my life to cleanse me and take control as my Lord.

By your Holy Spirit make me into the person You want me to be.

Amen.

Be prepared for some tears. Emotions are a God-given part of us and are appropriate in some situations. Give an opportunity for private conversation afterwards. In private, offer to pray with the person. They may choose to repeat the words of your prayer, aloud or in silence, or they may prefer to read a prayer, or say their own. The important thing is that if they want to make a relationship with God, they should talk to him.

Some like Penny may choose to go away and pray on their own, If so, encourage them to tell someone what they have done. Others may realise that they have become Christians previously and will benefit from being able to tell someone.

Have literature available for people to read or take home.

My commitment (Cliff College).

How to know God as Father (Bible Society).

Knowing God Personally (Campus Crusade for Christ).

Journey into Life (Falcon).

Bible reading booklets to encourage and aid Bible reading. (Scripture Union, Bible Reading Fellowship, *Every Day with Jesus* and others).

KEY POINTS TO REMEMBER

- ☐ God converts. We are the messengers.
- ☐ There is no place for pressure or intimidation here.
- ☐ The Holy Spirit has been at work in these people's lives already, bringing them to the point of decision.
- ☐ We need to make people aware that the Christian life is not a cop-out, an easy option, or an insurance policy. God requires our total commitment to himself, and that can be costly.

TO THINK ABOUT

- **Is it appropriate to offer a challenge to commitment in any small group I am involved in at the moment?**
- **Who should do it?**
- **What literature will we have available?**

Write down anything you intend to do about it.

8 NURTURE AND INTEGRATION

> "We shall become mature people, reaching to the very height of Christ's full stature" *Ephesians 4:13*

Danny became a Christian at a youth meeting at his friend's house when a visiting youth leader spoke to the group about the challenge of Christ to today's young people. He had only been to one previous Christian event, and that was a gospel rock concert in the local town. Danny was enthusiastic about his new-found faith, and went with his friend to church the following Sunday. He was warmly welcomed, and though he found a lot of what went on very puzzling he thought he could probably get the hang of it, given time. The following week people were needed to paint the main hall, and Danny went along, spending three evenings there. The week after that he had a visit from the Sunday School Superintendent asking if he would teach a class of 10 year old boys in the Sunday School. When he emerged from taking his very first class, a church member was waiting for him to ask if he would join the property committee ... And so it went on. Within 6 months Danny left the church, disillusioned, sapped of all enthusiasm, feeling used to the point of being abused – and no one had offered him any support, Christian counsel, encouragement or help.

What went wrong? How could the church have handled the situation better?

Danny's church did not appear to realise that the initial commitment to Christ is only a beginning. We are not seeking swift conversions to provide more workers in the church. We are seeking ongoing disciples for Jesus Christ, and that is the work of a lifetime.

For there to be growth there must be nurture. It is the Holy Spirit who does the work of sanctification in us, but the task of the church is to provide the environment in which that process can take place.

One-to-One Support

Every new Christian, and perhaps especially one who has not been brought up in the church, needs to talk to someone about it all on a regular basis. There will be questions, doubts, misunderstandings, joys and surprises to share.

Just as a new-born baby needs nurture, so does the new-born Christian and, for both, the care of a significant other person is vital if s/he is to grow.

The Small Group

Part of the nurture is provided by a small caring group.

For teaching the basics of the Christian faith

- God the Creator, man made in the image of God but fallen, Jesus, salvation, Holy Spirit, worship, service.

If a number of new Christians have come on the scene at the same time, a special group may be formed in which, with a more experienced leader, they can explore what it means to be a Christian. Nurture needs knowledge.

If there is only one new Christian, there is no harm in an established group going back to basics as a refresher course for the established members and a start for the new one.

For sharing thoughts, beliefs, doubts and experiences

Sharing one's personal history with a caring group is an affirming experience. We all have the need to *belong.* In a large church particularly, there is the danger of the individual feeling unheard, unappreciated and taken for granted unless there is opportunity within a small group situation to have these needs met.

Older Christians can share their personal history, too, but should avoid giving the impression that the Christian life is easy and trouble-free! There's no room for triumphalism or embellished success stories.

For praying together

Praying together is effective, strengthening, and aids concentration. At first it is hard to pray aloud in a group. We all recall the dry throat, tight chest, short breaths and jumbled words of our first attempts.The stumbling sincere prayers of someone new to it are doubtless more pleasing to God than any fluent but mindless prayers of the more experienced.

We can help people to articulate their first prayers by:-

- asking everyone, even the experienced, to say only one sentence.
- offering a simple formula for everyone to use. 'Father we thank you ... Amen'.
- asking each person to write a short sentence prayer, gather them together, and randomly hand them out to read aloud. No one will be embarrassed by reading their own prayer.
- passing round a selection of printed prayers to be used.
- asking members to bring a prepared prayer to read/say.

After the first time, it gets easier!

For preparation for membership

Membership preparation classes led by the minister or a lay person can provide the necessary groundwork for new Christians, and introduce them to the privileges and responsibilities of being a member of the Church.

For social action

Small groups are a useful base from which to engage in social action:-

- caring as a team in practical ways for local people.
- organising fund-raising efforts for worthwhile causes.
- organising displays or sales of Third World goods.
- lobbying MPs about local issues.
- jointly funding an overseas project.

Working together on something draws people into the life of the church, makes them feel needed and valued, and serves the Kingdom of God.

For evangelism

New Christians are good at it! They have the enthusiasm and have so recently been there that they can communicate effectively with those who have not yet faced the challenge of the gospel. They should not be hurtled into it too soon, before they are reasonably well grounded in the basics of faith, but it should not be left so long that they have forgotten how it used to be for them.

The Welcome in the Church

Church can be a culture shock! For those who have recently become Christians (and for those who have been at it a long time!) the church can pose problems.

The building

Note the points in chapter 1 about the message the appearance of the building gives.

The people

Should be:-

- welcoming but not overwhelming.
- prepared to make the first move.
- sensitive to different people's differing needs.
- prepared to listen more than talk.

A welcome meeting for new people could be held from time to time, at which several established church members have the opportunity to meet the new ones.

The worship

Should be:-

- easy to follow, with pointers to guide people through.
- free from jargon.

– free from unexplained happenings.
– clear about who is welcome to what.

Bible reading

Reading the Bible is one of the ways we learn what God is like, and what he requires of us. But it's long, in parts it's hard to understand, and many people are daunted by the thought of it.

There are many helps available:-

– Bible reading aids dated and undated for all ages.
– audio cassettes with passages of the Bible read aloud with comments.
– video cassettes which explore biblical themes.
– commentaries, maps.

For many people the Bible comes alive in the small group situation, where questions can be asked, points clarified and different interpretations and applications offered.

Prayer

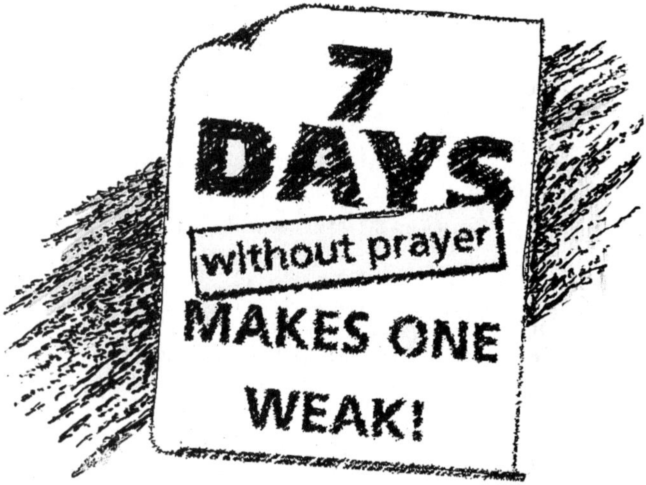

It's natural to communicate with those we love, but many of us find prayer difficult, perhaps because we have never been taught how to do it or heard of the variety of approaches available to us.

Prayer consists of talking to God and listening to him.

It includes:-

- praising God for who he is.
- saying sorry for the ways we have displeased God.
- thanking him.
- asking for things for others.
- asking for things for ourselves.

Reading printed prayers is helpful, and can lead on into our own prayers.

The psalms are a rich source of prayers. Prayer without words is a deep way of praying, simply communing with God, enjoying his company, offering situations or people to him without telling him what to do about them.

Books

For those with the incentive to read, there are many helpful books available for new Christians. Many a person's life has been transformed by the reading of a book.

A church bookstall can make a feature of a particular book, with recommendations in the magazine, reminders from the pulpit, and a large display to draw attention to it. People take notice if a book is recommended.

All members can be encouraged to read a particular book during Lent, or at any other period in the church calendar, with opportunity to meet in groups to discuss it.

Do not try to protect new Christians from books of a different theological outlook from your own; if they show interest, both of you read the book and discuss it together.

Service

There are responsibilities as well as privileges in being a Christian. The Methodist Covenant service says:

On the one side, God promises in the Covenant to give us new life in Christ. On the other side, we are pledged to live no more for ourselves but for him.

Inside the Methodist ticket of membership we read:

In the Church:

Members are committed to worship, holy communion, fellowship and prayer and bible study, responsible giving,

In the world:

Members are committed to the working out of their faith in daily life, service, the offering of personal service in the community, the Christian use of their resources, and the support of the Church in its total world mission.

The areas of service are wide! The church leadership and the new Christian will need to seek God's guidance. Sometimes enthusiasm to get involved and to serve will need restraining, at other times fanning into flame.

In the Church

Many people do not feel they belong unless they have a job to do. However, as in Danny's case, we need to beware of giving them too much too soon and with too little support!

Initially it can be helpful to have a newcomer working with someone else, enabling them to feel useful, to learn the job, and to discover whether it is the right one for them.

The church leadership has a great responsibility here to ensure that people are given tasks suited to their abilities, and that by doing them they are not prevented from using their special gifts.

When a person is given a responsibility, a clear and accurate job description should be offered, together with some idea how long the commitment is likely to be for, and what committee meetings are involved! They will appreciate ongoing support in the form of enquiries from time to time as to how it's going.

In the world

There are many forms of service in the community and the wider world, and Christians are doing excellent voluntary work in organisations such as:-

- Amnesty International.
- Samaritans.
- Relate.
- Local politics.
- Parent-teacher associations.

It is while they are expressing their faith in these fields that Christians find opportunities to speak about their beliefs to others.

KEY POINTS TO REMEMBER

☐ Do offer nurture to new Christians.

☐ Do let them take a lead as soon as they are ready.

☐ Don't ignore them or assume that they are getting on all right. Ask!

☐ Don't overload them.

TO THINK ABOUT

- **Who are the new Christians in my church and how might they be feeling?**
- **What provision has the church made to meet their needs?**
- **Should any new groups be set up for them?**
- **Should any established groups modify their programmes temporarily or permanently to cater for them?**
- **Is there a job I have in the church or outside which I could share with or offer to a newcomer?**

Write down anything you intend to do about it.

APPENDIX ONE

Ten series of brief outlines for Bible studies for people exploring faith

SERIES ONE: PARABLES OF THE KINGDOM

General questions for unpacking parables.
What is the main point of this parable?
Who/what represents whom/what?
What does the parable say to us?

Study 1. The Sower Matthew 13:1-9, 18-23

Prepare a wall/floor chart with the left-hand column filled in. Looking at the Bible passage all together, fill in columns 2 and 3.

Where seed fell	*What happened to it*	*Explanation*
Path	*(birds ate up)*	*(don't understand, Evil One snatches away*
Rocky ground	*(quick growth, scorched)*	*(give up when trouble comes)*
Thorns	*(choked)*	*(unfruitful because of worries)*
Good soil	*(good crop)*	*(hear, understand, fruitful)*

Make the following statements:

The seed is the message of the Kingdom.

The message is the good news that Jesus loves us, offers us forgiveness and new life in his Kingdom.

What sort of ground do we think we each are?

Where do we feel we are on the chart?

Study 2: Treasure and Pearl — Matthew 13:44-45

Ice-breaker

Imagine there is a fire at your house. Once the people are all out, you have time to collect only three things. What would they be?

Bible input

- What do you picture when you hear the words, 'Kingdom of heaven?' Does the idea appeal to you?
- Is the Kingdom of heaven mostly to do with the future or the here and now?
- In what sense, if any, is the Kingdom of heaven like a treasure or a pearl to you?
- The man in verse 44 stumbled upon the treasure accidentally. Is it possible to find the Kingdom of heaven accidentally?
- The merchant in verse 45 was looking for fine pearls. How would you suggest we look for the Kingdom of heaven?
- Both men sold everything. What might this mean in practice for people who find the Kingdom of heaven? Is it worth everything?
- How does the Kingdom of heaven compare in value for you with the three things you saved from your burning home?

Other suggestions for developing the theme

1. Write a postcard home from either of the men describing what has happened.
2. Re-write the two parables in a modern setting.

Study 3: The Tenants — Matthew 21:33-46

Ice-breaker

What sort of things strike you as being unfair? Think back to this week's news items. Discuss the suggestions offered: what is unfair about it? Who suffers? etc.

Bible input

- Prepare in advance a wall/floor chart with headings along the top:
  Landowner Tenants Slaves Son
- In small groups identify everything that is said about either the landowner, the tenants, the slaves or the son. Note them on chart.
- Who does the householder represent? The tenants? the slaves? the son? Note on chart.
- What point was Jesus making?
- What has that to do with us? Where might we fit in on the chart?
- Follow on with discussion about who killed Jesus, why, what we would have done if we had been there, how it makes us feel now, and anything we need to do about it.

Study 4: The lost son — Luke 15:11-32

Ice-breaker

Tell a modern story eg. daughter runs away from home, becomes pregnant, is welcomed back home, elder sister angry.
How would you feel as a) the mother b) the daughter c) the elder sister?

Bible input

- In small groups, using the Bible passage, discuss how either the father, the lost son or the elder brother would be feeling at each stage of the story.
- Who does the father represent? The lost son? the elder brother?
- Where do I fit in?
- What can we learn about God from this parable?

SERIES TWO: PEOPLE JESUS MET

The following questions can be used for all of these studies.
What do we learn about Jesus?

What do we learn about the person he met?

In what ways are we similar to or different from the person?

What can we learn from this incident?

In all these studies, if the group is comfortable with the idea, the passage can be read by group members taking parts. Otherwise, either read it yourself or tell the story before asking people to look at the detail.

Study 1: Nicodemus	John 3:1-16
Study 2: Woman at the well	John 4:1-38
Study 3: Man born blind	John 9:1-41
Study 4: Lazarus	John 11:1-44
Study 5: Centurion	Luke 7:1-10
Study 6: Simon the Pharisee	Luke 7:36-50

Further suggestions for developing any of these studies

1. Build up a character study of the person and of Jesus (cf studies on the life of Peter in Chapter Five).
2. In twos or with a panel of questioners, prepare and hold an interview with the person Jesus met in which he/she explains what happened, how it felt, and how they have changed as a result of meeting Jesus.
3. Think of a newspaper headline for the event.

SERIES THREE: SERMON ON THE MOUNT

Study 1: The Beatitudes — Matthew 5:1-12

Ice-breaker

The Be-Happy-Tudes
What makes us happy? Sad?

Bible input

- In twos, re-write each beatitude in today's language.
- Pool ideas and try to agree on a version for each.

For further discussion

1. Which, if any, of these is true for me?
2. Which would I want to be my experience?
3. Which would I feel most uncomfortable with?
4. Can people become like this if they want to? How? What stops them?

Study 2: The Lord's Prayer — Matthew 6:5-14

Ice-breaker

In small groups discuss the following questions, each group starting at a different question.

- What sort of situations make people pray?
- Which recent news items may have caused people to turn to prayer?
- Why do people pray in crises? What does that say about how they picture God?
- What is prayer?

Ask each group to offer to the whole group comments on the first question they looked at.

Bible input

- Read the Lord's prayer. What seem to be the main ingredients in this prayer? How do our prayers compare with this? What can we learn?

- Questions to think about:
  'Our' Whose?
  'Father' In what sense is God our Father?
  'In heaven' What do we mean by heaven?
  'honoured' (hallowed) Why?
  'your will be done on earth' Is it? Why/why not? Whose fault?
  'give us' Does he? Can he? Should we ask him to? Why/why not?
  'forgive us' Why should he? Does he? Are we forgiven automatically? What do we have to do?
  'as we forgive' Do we? Is it easy?
  'evil one' Who is he? What does he do? How can we escape him?

- Slowly, thoughtfully, say the Lord's prayer together.

Study 3: Ask, Seek, Knock — Matthew 7:7-14

Ice-breaker

Tell the story: A 5-year old boy asks his dad if he can take his dad's Stanley knife out to play with. Dad refuses. Son says dad cannot love him or else he would let him. If you were the dad would you:

a) give him the knife
b) give him a good hiding
c) send him to his bedroom
d) explain that it is dangerous
e) say nothing
f) or what?

Bible input

- From verses 9-11, what kind of picture is given of 'your Father in Heaven'? Is this the sort of Father you would want?

- Read verses 7-8. In the light of the kind of Father you have discovered in verses 9-11, what do you think 'ask and you will receive' means and does not mean?
- Do you think there is anything God would not give if you asked him for it?
- Have you any experience of not receiving something from God which you had asked him for?
- What do you think Jesus is referring to when he says, 'Seek, and you will find; knock and the door will be opened to you'?
- Is there anything you are seeking from God now? Is it for your ultimate good?

Study 4: Wise and Foolish Builders
Matthew 7:24-27

Ice-breaker

Tell the story: Two businessmen each had a new product to sell. One went straight into production, found there was no market for his product, and went bankrupt. The other spent a year doing market research, modified his product, and within 5 years of trading was a millionaire. Which would you rather support?

Bible input

- What are the similarities between the builders? What are the differences?
- Who does Jesus say is like the man who built his house on rock?
- Who does he say is like the man who built his house on sand?
- Notice that they both hear but only one obeys.
- In our lives, what does it mean to obey the words of Jesus?
- What are the rains, floods and winds in our lives? How does Jesus make a difference when things go wrong in our lives?

SERIES FOUR: EPHESIANS

Study 1: What God has done for us Ephesians 1:3-14

Ice-breaker

How do you feel when you receive a letter from a) a friend b) a member of your family c) your parliamentary candidate d) the taxman?

Bible input

- Read the passage in a good modern translation.
- List what it says God has done.
- How do you think the people in Ephesus would feel when they read this part of this letter?
- Which, if any, of these things are we each aware that God has done for us? How does it make us feel? How do we respond to it, if it's true?
- Spend some time quietly reading the list. Some may want to thank God for what he has done; some may want to acknowledge for the first time that they realise he has done it all for them.

Study 2: From death to life Ephesians 2:1-10

Ice-breaker

List as quickly as you can as many differences as you can think of between someone who is dead and someone who is alive.

Bible input

- Read the passage.

- What does the passage say about people a) before they become Christians? b) after they become Christians?
- What does it mean here to say that a person is 'dead'? (verse 1), 'alive'? (verse 5).
- What do you understand by grace? faith? (verse 8).
- Do we deserve God's grace? Do we need it? If so, what for?
- How do we know whether we have it?
- Where does faith come from? How do we know whether we have it?

N.B. Well-established Christians in the group should be encouraged only to make comments occasionally, and not to dominate the discussion; the aim is for the others to explore these ideas for themselves and come to their own conclusions.

Study 3: Christian living — Ephesians 4:17-32

Ice-breaker

Remind group members of adverts eg. carpet cleaners, washing powders, a local cleaners' shop, where there is a dramatic difference between the before and the after.

Bible input

- This passage is about the before and after of becoming a Christian. Make one list of the characteristics before, and another of what is expected after.
- What is the secret of living like this? (see verses 21-4, 32)
- What do you understand by the words, 'God in Christ forgave you' (verse 32)?
- Is this your experience?

Study 4: Christian armour Ephesians 6:10-20

Ice-breaker

Remind group members of battles between 'goodies' and 'baddies' through the ages – David and Goliath, Cowboys and Indians, Cops and Robbers. This battle goes on for real between God and the powers of evil – although ultimately God has won the war through the death of Jesus on the Cross. It is a spiritual battle, and if we are on God's side we are in the thick of it.

Bible input

- What is the struggle against? How do we understand that?
- To what extent are we aware of being involved in a battle?
- We are instructed to equip ourselves for the battle. Notice that it is God who provides the armour.
- Consider each item of spiritual armour and discuss in small groups what each means: truth, righteousness, gospel of peace, faith, salvation, word of God.
- Do we feel adequately equipped for a spiritual battle?

SERIES FIVE: THE CRUCIFIXION

Study 1: Around the Cross Matthew 27:32-56, Luke 23:26-49, John 19:17-37

The following people are referred to around the Cross:- Simon of Cyrene, Robber 1, Robber 2, Passers-by, Chief Priests and Teachers of the law, Centurion, John, various named women. In groups of two or three, take one gospel account, identify one character or group, and read the incident standing as it were in their shoes; feel what they felt, express their thoughts, share insights.

All together talk about what insight you have gained, or else the leader ask a few questions of each group to identify the differing responses.

With whom, if any, do we identify?

An alternative approach

Watch the video *Good Friday* (10 minutes, cartoon drawings, simple narrative, music over. Available to buy or hire from Scripture Union) and follow it up with discussion about the characters.

Study 2: Words from the Cross

Before the meeting write up the words of Jesus from the Cross on a wall chart.

1. Luke 23:24	'Father, forgive ...'
2. Luke 23:43	'... in Paradise'
3. Matt 27:46	'My God ...'
4. John 19:26-7	'behold your son ...mother'
5. John 19:28	'I thirst'
6. Luke 23:46	'Into your hands ...'
7. John 19:30	'It is finished'

Discuss the meaning and significance of each. What sort of person do these words suggest that Jesus was? Was his death a failure or a success? What has it to do with us?

SERIES SIX: THE LIFE OF JESUS IN MARK'S GOSPEL

Study 1: His ministry: call, healing, teaching. Mark 1:14-20, 3:1-6, 12:28-34.

Ice-breaker

What do you think Jesus is best known for? List all suggestions. Underline any connected with followers, healing or teaching. Save the list for referral in studies 2 and 3.

Bible input

Read Mark 1:14-20

- What are the different parts of Jesus' message?
- What does each mean?
- What was there about Jesus and/or his message which could have attracted the fishermen?
- Does anything about the message or the man attract you?

Read Mark 3:1-6

- What range of feelings do you think Jesus went through during this incident?
- Why do you think some people opposed Jesus?
- Why did Jesus make the man stand up?
- Why did Jesus tell him to stretch out his hand, and not simply tell him that it was healed?
- Is there any act of faith which Jesus is calling you to make?

Read Mark 12:28-34

- What would it take for the teacher of the law to be in the Kingdom of heaven instead of just not far from it?
- Are there people today who know all the right answers but are not yet part of the Kingdom?

To draw the discussion together

What kind of picture of Jesus is unfolding?

Study 2: His death Mark 15:1-41 especially 21-41

Ice-breaker

Look back and see whether the death of Jesus was one of the well-known things you noted about him in Study 1.

Either tell the story of someone who gave his life so that others could live

Or show the video, *'The Only Son'* (14 minutes. Bishop of Iran tells how his only son was killed by revolutionaries. Available to buy or hire from Scripture Union).

Bible input

- See also *Series 5* Study 1.
- Read the passage.
- Why did Jesus die? Offer the following ideas to consider.
  1. He misjudged the support he would get.
  2. God planned it that way.
  3. The Jewish leaders needed him out of the way.
  4. The Jewish people did not realise who he was.

5. Judas was trying to force the hand of Jesus to make him take power from the Romans.

6. Jesus intended jumping off the Cross but found that he was too weak.

- Look again at verses 37-39. Explain that the ripping of the curtain was symbolic of opening the way to God for all. Verse 39. Do you agree with the centurion?
- If it was God who was on the Cross, what is the significance for us?

Study 3: His resurrection — Mark 16:1-8

Ice-breaker

Note whether resurrection was something you said in Study 1 that Jesus was best known for.

Either discuss the difference between resurrection and resuscitation

Or watch the video *Easter Sunday* (10 minutes, simple narrative, cartoon pictures, music over, to buy or hire from Scripture Union).

Bible Input

- Read Mark 16:1-8

  verses 1-4 What were the women expecting?

  verse 5 Why were they alarmed?

  verse 8 Why did they keep quiet?
- Imagine that you were there. Describe the incident to your grandchildren years later, saying how you felt and why.
- When Jesus appeared to many people later, what effect did it have on them? (See early chapters of Acts).
- Was Jesus resurrected or resuscitated?

Application

Why was Jesus raised? What difference can it make to us? (See 1 Corinthians 15 for further study).

SERIES SEVEN: THE EARLY CHURCH IN THE ACTS OF THE APOSTLES

General questions for exploring the suggested passages in the Acts of the Apostles

- What can we learn from this passage about God the Father? God the Son, God the Holy Spirit? Humankind?
- Is there a command to obey?
  an error to avoid?
  a promise to hold on to?
  a warning to heed?
  an example to follow?
- What motivated the apostles in the first place?
- What kept them going?
- Do these things happen today?

Other approaches

1) Much of Acts lends itself to dramatisation, role play or interview. Be sure that if you use any of these methods you allow sufficient time for group members to talk about what the passage says to them.
2) Work out character studies of some of the apostles from the suggested passages.
3) Watch the video *The Holy Spirit* in the *Jesus Then and Now* series. (20 minutes, interviews, drama, comment. Available to buy or hire from Scripture Union).

Study passages

Study 1: Acts 2:1-13, 22-24, 32-42
Study 2: Acts 3:1-20
Study 3: Acts 9:1-18
Study 4: Acts 16:16-40
Study 5: Acts 19:1-10

Sample

Study 2: A Lame Man is Healed

1. Tell the story of verses 1-9
   What would we have thought if we had been there?
2. Read verse 11
   What would you expect Peter to do next?
3. All read silently verses 12-20
   According to Peter, who was responsible for the miracle?
4. On a prepared chart, fill in Peter's statements under the headings:- What God did. What you did. What you must do. What the result will be.

Application

How can/does this apply to us?

SERIES EIGHT: OLD TESTAMENT CHARACTERS

Study 1: Abraham

Aim
To note the depth of Abraham's faith in and knowledge of God, and to compare it with ours.

Bible input

Based on Genesis chapters 12-18, 20-23, 25 verses 1-11. Focusing on God's call to him and testing of him.

The study
Leader: first, briefly tell Abraham's life story.
The call. ***Read aloud Genesis 12:1-9.***
Abraham took a step of faith.
What sort of things could have held him back? What would we have done in his circumstances?

The testing: ***Read Genesis 22:1-19***

Abraham trusted God.

Application

Do we know God well enough to trust him as much as this? How can we get to know him?

Study 2: Joseph

Aim

To show that Joseph believed that God was in every situation, however bad it seemed at the time, and that he was able to forgive his brothers.

Bible input

Based on Genesis chapters 37, 39 and 40-45.

Focusing on his relationship with his brothers.

The study

Leader: first, briefly tell Joseph's life story.

● ***Read Genesis 45: 1-9, 50: 15-21.***

What was Joseph's reaction to what his brothers had done to him? Is that the reaction you would have expected?

Application

If you had endured the same as Joseph, would you have been able

a) to say that God did it, and he meant it for good? Look up Romans 8:28 where St Paul says something similar.

b) to forgive your brothers?

If we know we are forgiven by God does that help us to forgive other people? How can we receive God's forgiveness?

An alternative approach

Watch the video *Joseph* (in four episodes: Dreamer 17 minutes, Slave 16 minutes, Prisoner 16 minutes, Governor of Egypt 21 minutes. Available to buy or hire from Scripture Union).

Study 3: Moses

Aim

To show that, like many other people, Moses made excuses when God called him.

Bible input

● ***Read Exodus chapter 3 to chapter 4 verse 17***

God gave Moses a clear sign of his presence in the burning bush, and then he called him to serve him.

● What excuses did Moses make?

● How did God respond to each?

Application

In what ways does God make his presence felt to us?

What does he call us to do?

What excuses do we offer?

Do you think God has an answer to your excuses?

An alternative approach

Watch the video *Exodus.* (in five episodes: Slaves 15 minutes, *Fighting Back* 11 minutes, *Let my people go* 13 minutes, *Battle of wills* 13 minutes, *The way of no escape* 13 minutes. Available to buy or hire from Scripture Union).

Study 4: Joshua

EITHER

Aim

To show that Joshua is the kind of leader whose example we might like to follow.

Bible input

- ***Read Joshua chapters 1,5,6,10,23,24***
- Leader: tell the story of Joshua highlighting the incidents in these chapters.
- List the aspects of his character which you admire.

Application

Does what he said and did make you want to serve the Lord he served? Is there anything stopping you?

OR

Aim

To show that choices have to be made.

Bible input

- ***Read Joshua 24:14-27***
- What choices were open to the Israelites?
- What made them want to serve the Lord?
- What were they told to do about foreign gods?

Application

What might make it difficult for you to choose to serve the Lord?
What would make you want to choose to serve him?
What is the equivalent of the 'foreign gods' in your life?

SERIES NINE: PSALMS

Study 1: Psalm 24

Read the psalm. This may be done with the leader or one group asking the questions, the others making the statements. Ensure that all are using the same translation.

Discuss what the psalm says about God. Is that our experience of him?

Discuss what the psalm says God looks for in his people. Does that describe us, or not?

When we fall short of God's standards, he has provided a way for us to become acceptable to him. Read John 3:16. What do we need in order to be acceptable to God?

Study 2: Psalm 32

Ice-breaker

Give each person a newspaper and ask them to select two or three articles which illustrate something about human nature, good or bad.

Identify how many of the selected articles illustrate something good about human nature, and how many something bad.

Discuss what seems to be wrong with human nature (greed, selfishness, cruelty, etc). Are we the same, or different from this? What do you think God feels about the way humans treat each other?

Bible input

● ***Read Psalm 32***

- What does the psalmist say are the results of a) having our sins forgiven? b) having unforgiven sin?

Application

Is this our experience or not?

Comment that we have a big advantage over the psalmist because we know that Jesus died so that we could be forgiven, have peace with God and therefore be able to have peace of mind.

Do we feel the need of forgiveness today? If we do, what can we do about it?

Study 3: Psalm 51:1-12

David wrote this psalm after Nathan had challenged him about his sin in taking Bathsheba and murdering her husband. (2 Samuel 11).

Bible input

- Read verses 1-12, counting how many times the words *'me', 'my'* and *'I'* occur.
- How is David feeling about himself?
- What does David want God to do for him? Does he feel he deserves it?

Application

David knew that religion is a personal relationship between the individual and God. Is that our understanding?

How important is forgiveness in our lives?

What do we need to do to be forgiven by God?

SERIES TEN: CHRISTIAN FESTIVALS

Study 1: Advent and Christmas

Ice-breaker

What do most people in this country think that Christmas is about? What do you think it is about? Why do many people spend a lot of time and money preparing for it?

Bible input

● ***Read Matthew 1:18-25***

Why do you think God decided that Jesus would be born to an ordinary, humble person?

Do you think Jesus was God, or man, or both? Why?

● ***Read John 1:1-5***

What strikes you as most interesting, surprising or exciting in these verses?

● ***Read 2 Corinthians 5:19***

What does it mean, that God was in Christ, reconciling the world to himself?

Application

What difference would it make to you if Jesus had not been born?

Study 2: Lent and Easter

Ice-breaker

What does Easter mean to most people in this country? What does it mean to you? Do many people today take any notice of Lent? Why/why not?

Bible input

See SERIES 5, Studies 1 and 2 and SERIES 6, Study 3 in this Appendix.

Study 3: Pentecost

Ice-breaker

Describe, act out or draw the strongest power you have ever encountered in your life. Let others guess what it is.

Bible input

- ***Read Acts 2:1-15, 36-39***
- What do you think happened?
- What was the effect (i) on the disciples? (ii) on the people who listened to Peter?

Application

Can we be filled with the Holy Spirit? How? When? What difference would we expect him to make?

Is there anything we need to do about it now?

APPENDIX TWO

FOR FURTHER READING

On Evangelism

Small Group Evangelism Richard Peace *IVP 1985*

Family Evangelism John Hattam *Scripture Union Missions Dept 1989*

Making Adult Disciples Anton Baumohl *Scripture Union 1984*

Good News Down the Street Michael Wooderson *Grove booklet*

The Church Down Our Street Michael Wooderson *MARC 1989*

The Good News Works Ed. G. Howard Mellor *Methodist Home Mission Division 1991*

On small groups

Headway with Housegroups *Methodist Division of Ministries 1982*

Leading Groups: A Training Course Margaret Parker *Epworth 1987*

Growing Christians in Small Groups John Mallison *Scripture Union 1989*

Good Things Come in Small Groups Foreword by Roy Pointer *Scripture Union 1987*

God at Work in Small Groups Albert J Wollen *Scripture Union 1983*